Gunnersbury Park
The Place and the People

What brings people to Gunnersbury Park?
Millions have played here with their children,
walked their dogs, strolled through quiet areas,
competed in energetic sports, bought teas
and ice creams in the café. Everyone has their
own experience, making their own memories.
Discovering Gunnersbury's past, seeing its
landscape and buildings in new ways, can enrich
every visit.

1

From Manor House to Maynard

The south-facing slopes enjoy sunshine from dawn to dusk. The views of the Thames valley, and of London to the east, can be breathtaking. Open skies in London are now hard to find – looking west from the field can be inspirational. The Bath Road and the Uxbridge Road linked London and the west, while the old rural track from Ealing Common towards Brentford and Kew can still be followed through the grounds. For much of its life, Gunnersbury has been the home of wealthy Londoners.

The fertile soils of Middlesex created valuable farmland. A line of springs along the north of the estate and in Potters Field, across today's Popes Lane, supplied fresh water. That field name, like the neighbouring Clayponds estate, offers a clue to the significance of the local clay which, along with deposits of gravel, sand and brickearth, provided valuable raw materials. The bricks for the 17th-century mansion, and for some of the walls still standing, were probably made on the estate.

OPPOSITE Maynard's mansion; a view from the south across rich farmland bathed in golden sunshine. Watercolour by William Payne, 1792.

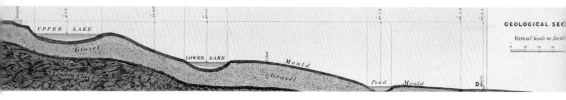

The land here was so valuable that Christian Saxon kings used it to fund their new Diocese of London and St Paul's Cathedral. Although given to the Bishop of London in 701 as part of the manorial estate of Ealing, the place name is first recorded in 1347. It was named after a former owner, Gunhilda, a woman's name which was common locally in the 13th century. Edward III's mistress, Alice Perrers, was granted the lease in 1373. Though one of the wealthiest landowning women in England, her extravagance, strong influence upon the king and alliance with corrupt courtiers led to her impeachment in 1376 and her land was confiscated.

From the legal battles over that land in the next two years comes the earliest description we have of Gunnersbury. A panel of jurors stated that Alice paid 36 shillings and 8 pence in quarterly instalments to the bishop for her 228-acre manor of Gonyldesberg. The dwelling house had adjoining yards, gardens and other buildings, and a ruined dove-house. The 140 acres of arable land were valued at 46 shillings and 8 pence a year; of these 30 acres were sown with corn, the crop worth 2 shillings an acre.

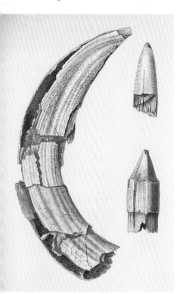

ABOVE Cross section from Kretschmar's 1847 survey, showing gravels over London Clay, along a line through the Round Pond and Horseshoe Pond. © Her Majesty Queen Elizabeth II 2018.

BELOW LEFT Prehistoric elephant tusk from Coles Hole, now the Potomac Lake. Brentford brickmaker William Kirby Trimmer's account of these finds appeared in the Royal Society's Journal in 1813. Engraved by James Basire. © The Royal Society.

ABOVE Robinson's Brentford Pottery, producing chimneypots, flowerpots, garden urns and forcing jars using Coles Hole clay. Oil painting, about 1845.

The land sown with wheat and rye gave a crop worth only 18 pence an acre because it had been sown in rainy weather; also many acres had recently been flooded.

Another 80 acres of pasture were worth annually 13 shillings and 4 pence and there were some cattle. Four acres of meadow were valued at 6 shillings. Four acres of wood had been cut down the previous year so that land was then worth nothing. The estate also rented out a house with two acres of land in Brentford.

OPPOSITE Sir John Maynard in legal robes, probably painted by Henry Tilson. Maynard's descendants took this portrait to Blickling Hall, Norfolk, where it is today.

FAR RIGHT Sir John Spelman and his wife Elizabeth, née Frowyck, who inherited Gunnersbury in 1522. Memorial brass in Narborough Church, Norfolk.

BELOW Henry Frowyck of Gunnersbury, alderman for the Basing Hall ward. He was Lord Mayor of London 1435–36.

The Frowyck family held the property by 1390 and retained it through inheritance and marriage until the 1580s. The family were London merchants, Lord Mayors, MPs, lawyers and judges; some were knighted. It passed through a daughter in 1522 to the Spelmans, another family of lawyers and judges. From 1582 until the 1650s, the ownership of the estate is hard to trace.

Despite the prominence of these families we have little evidence about their house and farm buildings. The upper slopes with the freshwater springs probably offered the best location. From the remaining medieval manor houses in Middlesex we can assume the dwelling house was probably timber framed, close studded, infilled with wattle and daub and thatched. As brick and tile became more affordable, it is likely that any alterations and additions over the centuries were made in these materials. In 2014 archaeological excavations revealed footings and drains in the north-east corner of the Park constructed from brick dating from 1470 to 1520. However, a large slice of land in this area was taken for the construction of the North Circular Road in the 1920s, so if this was the site, much has been lost.

Sir John Maynard, wealthy lawyer and West Country MP, owned the estate by 1654; his first wife died that December and she was buried in Ealing. A leading lawyer during the English Civil War and under Cromwell, he sustained his position under Charles II, receiving his knighthood in 1660. He had remarried in 1656 and between 1658 and 1663 transformed the estate with a fashionable Palladian

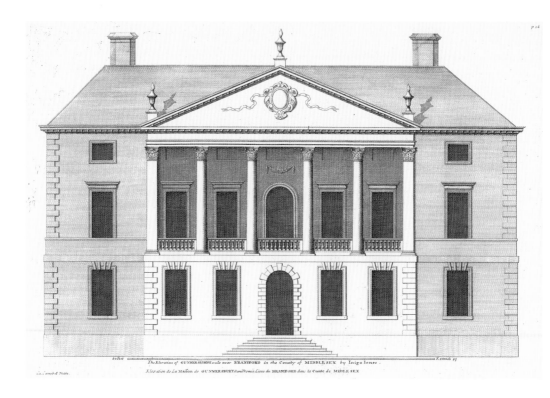

The Elevation of GUNNERSBURY House near BRANTFORD in the County of MIDDLESEX by Inigo Jones.
Elevation de La Maison de GUNNERSBURY demi Lieue du BRANTFORD dans la Comté de MIDLE SEX

mansion inspired by the Villa Badoer and designed by John Webb, Inigo Jones' assistant.

Assessed as having 44 hearths for the 1666 Hearth Tax, Maynard's Gunnersbury House was by far the biggest house in the area. To create a rectangular plot for his new house and gardens he diverted Gunnersbury Lane with two right-angled bends, the old road line becoming the axis of a symmetrical plan. A long section of his boundary wall of plum-red local brick, restored in 2016, runs parallel to the A406 from the grotto to the mock ruins near the Stables, another forms the back wall of the Orangery and a stretch survives within the Large Mansion's kitchen wing.

ABOVE The garden front. Engraving from *Vitruvius Britannicus*, 1715.

BELOW A plum-red brick from Maynard's garden wall, made from local clay, about 1660.

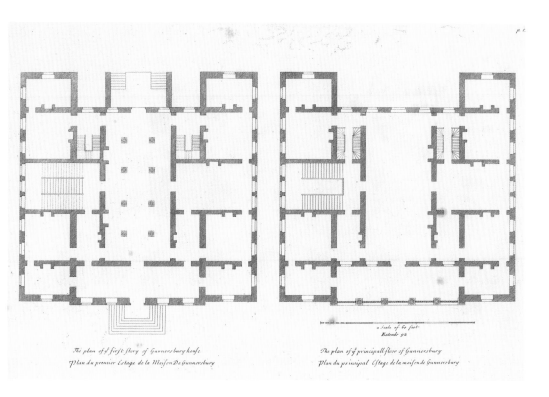

The plan of ʃ firʃt ʃtory of Gunnersbury houʃe
Plan du premier Estage de la Maiʃon De Gunnersbury

a ʃcale of 60 feet
Estendr 92

The plan of ʃ principall floor of Gunnersbury
Plan du principal Estage de la maiʃon de Gunnersbury

ABOVE Plans of the entrance level (left) and principal floor with the saloon and portico (right). Engraving from *Vitruvius Britannicus*, 1715.

Positioned at almost the highest point on the estate, the garden front of the new red-brick mansion with its white stone columns and pediment was visible for miles around. Guests would arrive through the entrance on the north side before progressing through a series of smaller rooms and a large vestibule with columns on the ground floor. They would then ascend the grand staircase into the massive central Saloon on the first floor, and make their way through to the balcony of the portico to admire the view down to the valley of the Thames and up to the hills of Richmond in the distance. (Today's equivalent viewpoint is from the upper floors of the Museum.)

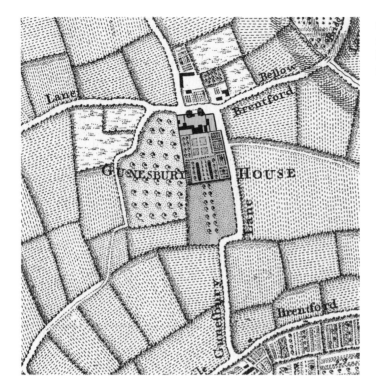

LEFT Detail from Rocque's 1746 map, with the levels of Maynard's house, gardens and paddock identified in modern colours.

The site was divided into three levels within a boundary wall. The house, outbuildings and perhaps two lodges facing the lane stood on the highest level, supported by a concealed brick revetment along the southern edge. Today's two mansions stand close to the edge of this terrace. Steps from the mansion led down to the next level, where four grass squares divided by gravel paths were flanked by a small orchard and an enclosed kitchen garden.

On the next level the central area had two long, parallel rectangular lakes with a central path lined with topiary and small trees either side; on the west was probably a flower garden and on the east two square beds each with

an ornamental tree in the middle. Beyond and below the southern wall, the central path continued as a tree-lined avenue through a grassy paddock. The two oldest trees in the park, two yews dating from 1650 to 1740, still stand among the humps and bumps of this southern wall.

This palatial mansion was designed for entertaining but it was also a home. In his last years Maynard worked on trunks of legal papers in his study at the east end of the portico. He was appointed a Commissioner of the Great Seal in 1689 and died in 1690 aged 88. His body lay in state at the mansion for two weeks in a lavish coffin, surrounded by painted heraldic drapery and pennants, before an expensive funeral at St Mary's Ealing. His memorials are his collection of manuscript law reports at Lincoln's Inn and his gift in 1682 of eight chests of books to enrich Harvard University Library.

Maynard's will created such a complex trust that it took nearly 50 years before his great-grandson, Sir John Hobart, could obtain an Act of Parliament allowing the sale of the estate and mansion to the highest bidder, by which time they had fallen into disrepair. Over the following 50 years, two wealthy owners transformed Gunnersbury.

ABOVE A John Webb overmantel from Gunnersbury, about 1660, inserted into an 18th-century interior at Milton Manor in Oxfordshire.

RIGHT Fine stone steps, reused near the gothic screen, may be the work of Edward Marshall, master mason on Maynard's Gunnersbury House.

2

'THE SALOON, 25 FEET HIGH, HAS AN
ENTRANCE INTO THE PORTICO AND IS A
DELIGHTFUL SITUATION IN THE AFTERNOON
IN THE WARM MONTHS IN SUMMER'

(W. Angus, *Seats of the Nobility and Gentry*, 1787)

Georgian Gunnersbury

Henry Furnese (c.1690–1756) bought 14 acres with the house and gardens in December 1739, with another 274 acres of farmland, most let to tenant farmers. The price was £12,700. A rich merchant trading through Portugal, he had inherited wealth from his father, an East India Company merchant, and from a cousin who had died in 1735. He was also an MP, mainly for the family seat of New Romney. Furnese lived in some luxury; outstanding bills at his death included £36 to the peruke-maker, £43 to Paul Crespin, silversmith, and £61 to Bryant Barrett the lace-maker.

A lover of music, Furnese sponsored performances of Handel's works and invited him to stay at Gunnersbury in 1754. Furnese's only written bequest was £5,000 to one of Handel's favoured sopranos, La Francescina.

Daniel Defoe wrote in 1742 of the double height central Saloon: 'This Room the present Possessor, Henry Furnese, Esq, is fitting up in a most elegant Taste; and he is possessed

OPPOSITE The view from Furnese's Temple, Gunnersbury's highest point. Two men on the Round Pond are paying out a fishing net from a punt, while a woman may have brought food for the gardeners in her bag. Watercolour by William Payne, 1792.

of a fine Collection of capital Pictures'. This collection, with works by Poussin, Canaletto and Rembrandt, was displayed against 192 yards of luxurious crimson silk damask from Genoa. Perhaps the £55 Furnese paid to William Kent in 1743 was for advice on this interior, as Kent had previously used similar damask at Kensington Palace and Hampton Court. Furniture was commissioned from specialist cabinet-makers William Vile and John Cobb and sculpture from John Carter.

It had become fashionable to remodel formal gardens using the inspiration of Italian Renaissance garden design and Virgil's Arcadia. John Rocque began his survey of *London*

ABOVE Nicolas Poussin's *Mars and Venus* was lot 55 in the auction of Furnese's pictures, sold for £105, the second most expensive work in the sale. Photograph © 2018 Museum of Fine Arts, Boston.

Gunnersbury.

and Environs in 1741, and his plan of Gunnersbury suggests that Maynard's garden had hardly changed in the 80 years since it was laid out. However, by the time the survey was published in 1746, Furnese would already have started his changes. Kent's letters to Lord Burlington mention three visits in 1744 and 1745. He knew Furnese socially and he stayed at Gunnersbury for 'the aire and company', to help him recover when he was not well. Daniel Lysons wrote in 1795 that the gardens had been enlarged and altered by Kent for Furnese. Certainly by 1765 43 acres of farmland had become his park, within which Furnese had built the Temple, recorded in the sales inventory after his death. As it makes a single composition with the Round Pond, Kent probably advised on both, and on planting cedars to create the setting.

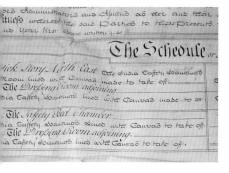

The print of 1761 suggests that Furnese remodelled some of his garden walls with a scalloped profile to imitate more closely those of the Villa Badoer. This work most likely led to the conversion of the formal lakes into the Horseshoe Pond, and the opening of a larger gateway in the southern boundary wall.

After a brief term in government office, Furnese died in August 1756. His sister, Elizabeth Pierce, inherited his estate but died in 1758, before she had sorted out his affairs. Disputes between the heirs led to a court judgement in 1761 ordering the sale of everything. The probate accounts record the cost of managing the estate as well as sales to resolve the debts. In addition to farms leased to tenants, they show that Furnese was farming some of his own land.

For example, in April 1762 *The Public Advertiser* announced the auction of Furnese's 'genuine rich and elegant Household Furniture, on site' including 14 very large pier glasses or mirrors, Persia and Turkey carpets, brewhouse equipment, garden tools, 'mellon frames and glasses, a tent and a markee, 80 fine Orange, Citron and Bergamot trees in tubs' and 'Carp, Perch, Tench, etc', probably from the Round Pond. Two dozen hams from Malaga, perhaps from his Portuguese trading, were also sold.

Princess Amelia's trustees bought Gunnersbury House, 15 acres of formal gardens and 43 acres of parkland, for £9,000 in 1762. The second daughter of George II, she had lived at Richmond Park as its Ranger from 1751. There she caused outrage by closing off public access and curtailing traditional rights to gravel, wood and water. A court judgement in 1758 went against her, ladder stiles were constructed over the walls to reinstate the right of way and she left in disgust in 1760. With a town house in Cavendish Square, Gunnersbury was now to be her country retreat for the rest of her life, close to her nephew, George III, and his family at Kew, many of whose portraits she displayed at Gunnersbury.

Amelia enjoyed manly pursuits such as fishing and horse-riding and dressed accordingly. She once shocked those at the chapel at Hampton Court by turning up 'in riding clothes with a dog under her arm', according to Horace Walpole,

BELOW Portrait of Princess Amelia (1711–1786). Oil painting on canvas after the portrait by Jean-Baptiste van Loo, about 1738. © Her Majesty Queen Elizabeth II 2018.

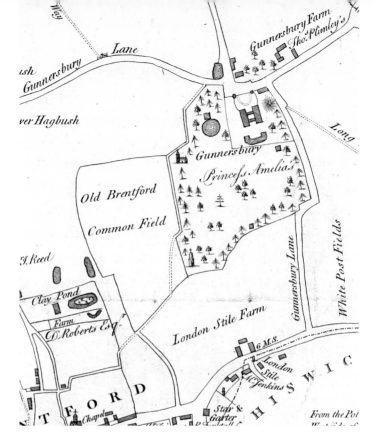

who also commented that she was 'an excellent mistress to her servants, steady to her favourites and nobly generous and charitable'. We know from the letters and diaries of her friends, Horace Walpole and Lady Mary Coke, that she loved evenings spent gambling at cards. This was also, however, a palace where she could throw fabulous and memorable parties. Indignant at George III's inhospitable treatment of the young King Christian VII of Denmark, her nephew-in-law, in 1768 she invited 300 of the nobility to Gunnersbury and offered a supper of 120 dishes, a spectacular firework display, and a ball which lasted until three in the morning.

She constructed a private chapel linked to the west side of the mansion and employed her own chaplain. She acquired additional farmland in 1770 and 1785. According to Daniel Lysons she spent over £20,000 on plantations and pavilions in the gardens. The pavilions around her perimeter walk have been lost, but we do still have the grotto she built in rustic brickwork against the estate wall, a pool with water tumbling in through a spout in a wall decorated with seashells.

Gunnersbury House proved hard to sell after Amelia's death in 1786. Her executors had been advised that it was worth £18,500, but in May 1788 Colonel Gilbert Ironside bought it and 125 acres at auction for what the press described as 'the very low sum of £9,050'. He had returned from 37 years' service in India in 1786, wealthy but in very poor health. A cultured man, he had sent seeds from India to botanist Dr John Fothergill and samples of Bengali earth to Josiah Wedgwood to use in ceramic experiments. His poor health probably prevented him from investing in the ageing mansion and in 1792 he sold Gunnersbury, retiring to his town house in Brook Street where he died aged 66 in 1802.

ABOVE LEFT Ink sketch of pavilion with a spire, perhaps shown on the 1777 map near the site of today's children's playground.

ABOVE RIGHT Ink sketch of pavilion with four columns, perhaps shown at the centre of the southern boundary on the 1777 map.

RIGHT Particulars for the unsuccessful 1787 auction of villa, chapel, gardens, pleasure grounds, hothouses, icehouse and farmland.

BELOW Proposal for a garden temple at Gunnersbury. Ink and colourwash, probably by John Oldfield, Princess Amelia's surveyor, who designed all the buildings erected during her ownership.

THE   XXXIV. 17703 60

P A R T I C U L A R S

OF THE CAPITAL

V I L L A,

WITH ADEQUATE

ATTACHED AND DETACHED OFFICES,

A neat Chapel, Fore Courts, Gardens, Terrace, Lawns and Pleasure Grounds,

Refreshed by a noble CANAL and FISH-POND,

Green-house, Pinery, Hot-houses, Ice-house, and a Shrubbery Walk,

Encompassing a rich PADDOCK, and Four contiguous MEADOWS,

THE WHOLE

One Hundred and Twenty-nine Acres, One Rood, and Five Perches,

BE THE SAME MORE OR LESS,

Most delightfully situate on that beautifully elevated SPOT

G U N N E R S B U R Y,

A SMALL DISTANCE FROM

KEW AND EALING, IN MIDDLESEX

THE LATE RESIDENCE OF

Her Royal Highnefs the PRINCESS AMELIA,

𝕯 𝕰 𝕮 𝕰 𝖆 𝕾 𝕰 𝕯:

Which will be S O L D by A U C T I O N,

By MR. *S K I N N E R* and *Co.*

On M O N D A Y the 7th of M A Y, 1787,

At Eleven o'Clock,

O N   T H E   P R E M I S E S,

BY ORDER OF THE EXECUTORS.

☞ On MONDAY *the 14th of* MAY, *and the Five following Days, at Eleven o'Clock, the rich* HOUSE-HOLD FURNITURE, *magnificent* PIER GLASSES *of large Dimensions,* FRENCH COMMODES *of exquisite Workmanship, most elegantly decorated with chased and engraved* Or Molu, SILK DAMASK HANGINGS, *a few capital* PICTURES, *Marble* BUSTOS *by* Rysbrack, *Two noble Stone* GROUPS, *fine old* Japan, Dresden, Chelsea, Salopian, *and* Oriental PORCELAIN, *brilliant cut* LUSTRES, *capital Green-house* PLANTS, *Stock of old* BEER, *and numerous* VALUABLE EFFECTS.

The VILLA, GROUNDS, &c. to be viewed between the Hours of Eleven and Four, by Tickets, which may be had, with printed Particulars, of Mr. SKINNER and Co. Alderfgate Street.

The EFFECTS to be viewed Four Days preceding the Sale, Sunday excepted ; but, *to prevent improper Company,* no Person can be admitted without a *Catalogue,* which may be then had on the Premifes, or in Alderfgate Street, for One Shilling—*to be returned to Purchafers.*

Five beautiful watercolours of Gunnersbury were commissioned from the fashionable artist, William Payne, in 1792. His romantic views of the estate show rich farmland and gardens bathed in sunlight. Though Amelia had added land and garden pavilions, the mansion was well over 100 years old, its condition was probably declining and London

ABOVE View east along the terrace. The domed pavilion on the icehouse mound gave a view towards Chiswick. Watercolour by William Payne, 1792.

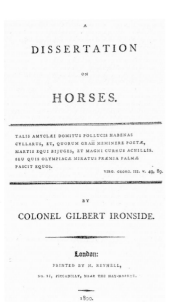

ABOVE *A Dissertation on Horses* by Colonel Ironside, written in his retirement and published in 1800. Part of the quotation from Virgil translates as 'If you want to win the Olympic palm, breed horses'.

RIGHT A scene Amelia would have known – a pleasure boat floats on the Horseshoe Pond and sheep graze the sloping lawns. *The Seat of Walter Stirling*, engraving by W. Angus, 1797.

was getting closer. If Ironside commissioned these pictures, perhaps it was because he knew this Arcadia could not last.

Walter Stirling of Faskine, Lanarkshire, described in the deeds as 'of the Navy Office', paid £10,500, supported by an £8,000 mortgage from Josiah Wedgwood. Money was obviously tight. In 1794 he opened negotiations to sell to his brother-in-law, Andrew Stirling, a London merchant, but did not complete the contract. In 1795 he did the same with Henry Crawford, formerly an East India Company official in Madras. In 1796 Crawford moved in and he finally bought the estate in 1800, reimbursing Wedgwood's mortgage and paying the balance of £3,025 to Walter and Andrew Stirling. Crawford immediately sold to John Morley, a manufacturer of floorcloth. Morley had recently bought The Grove estate in Carshalton, demolished Stone Court and sold parts of the estate; now he planned a similar treatment for Gunnersbury.

Gunnersbury House *in Middlesex, the Seat of* Walter Stirling Esq.r

3

'UPWARDS OF 80 ACRES OF LAND WITHIN
ONE WALL, MOST ADMIRABLY SUITED FOR
BUILDING ...'

(Advertisement in *The Times*, 12 May 1800)

Regency and Victorian Gunnersbury

The estate was divided. In May 1800 Morley advertised for sale building materials from the demolished mansion – Westmorland slate, Portland stone, mahogany doors and window glass – and offered the 83 acres in nine plots. The architect, John Soane, began designing himself a villa on one of them, but in the end purchased Pitzhanger Manor. Morley next offered 13 smaller plots, and in 1801 he sold Plot 1 to Stephen Cosser, a timber merchant and Plot 2 to Alexander Copland, a building contractor. Copland also bought Plots 12 and 13 which blocked Cosser's expansion and obtained Morley's agreement not to use the unsold land for brick production. Captain William Raven bought Plots 3 and 4 in 1802.

The wall built between Plots 1 and 2 divided the Horseshoe Pond, so Cosser and Copland agreed to manage the water supply from Potters Field to their shared lake. By June 1802 both families had moved into their new villas.

OPPOSITE View from the west showing that Copland's mansion originally had bow windows, matching those on Cosser's house. Watercolour, about 1830.

Stephen Cosser built Gunnersbury House (today's Small Mansion), the elegant two-storey villa which is still recognisable within the later additions. Between its bow windows runs a verandah, trimmed with Chinese-style bells along the eaves. Elements of the interior, such as some Soane-influenced vaulted ceilings, suggest a man of taste. He retained the existing buildings at the north-east corner to provide stables and a home for the gardener who managed the 6½ acres of gardens and pleasure grounds.

Cosser, an Edinburgh-born timber merchant and builder, owned a substantial timber wharf on the Thames at Millbank. When he died in 1806 at the age of 51, his son from his first marriage, Walter, inherited both the business and Gunnersbury, and sold the house on to a Major Morison.

Alexander Copland built Gunnersbury Park House (today's Large Mansion) on Plot 2. Born in 1774, he was apprenticed to surveyor Richard Holland, whose son, Henry, became his business partner. Through his mother he was related to the

ABOVE Stephen Cosser, Justice of the Peace and a Major in the Westminster Volunteer Cavalry. Miniature portrait by William Wood, about 1800.

LEFT Cosser's Millbank wharf, stacked high with timber (left) and his row of six houses. Detail from Daniel Turner's oil painting, *Lambeth Palace from the West*, 1802.

Smirke family of architects. Aged 22, Copland married Lucy Giffard, a lawyer's daughter from Turnham Green.

With £10,000 inherited from his builder father he made his fortune constructing prefabricated timber barracks and undertaking major contracts such as the Royal Military College at Sandhurst (1807–12) and the Theatre Royal, Covent Garden (1808–09) designed by his cousin, Robert Smirke. He purchased the Duke of York's Piccadilly mansion for £37,000 in 1802 and in partnership with Henry Holland converted it into Albany, London's first block of residential apartments. His wealth brought him a town house in St Martin's Lane and an aristocratic style of life, building his country house at Gunnersbury, putting on entertainments and riding to hounds.

RIGHT This plan with 13 new plots and a new east–west access road was displayed at Christie's auction house and included in parchment sale deeds.

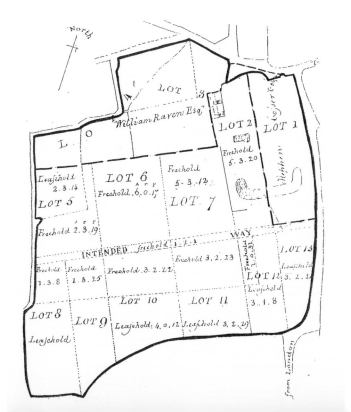

Copland acquired a 10,000 square yard site in Horseferry Road where he set up workshops, sawpits and brick stacks, only a short walk from Cosser's wharf. They probably knew each other when they planned their new homes at Gunnersbury.

Captain Raven was Copland's neighbour to the north-west. He was 46, with a new wife, when he bought 12¼ acres in Plots 3 and 4 in February 1802. He acquired the 18th-century walled garden, which he let to nurseryman Samuel Poupart, the Round Pond and the 'Dairy House', formerly Furnese's Temple, now converted into a two- storey house with a basement.

Though wounded as a young man in the Navy, Raven became captain of the *Britannia* carrying supplies between London and Australia. Back in London he became an official of Trinity House. The Captain kept a main home in Hackney, and then in Camberwell. He let his Gunnersbury property in 1808 to a Colonel Stapleton and in 1810 leased it to Copland.

Copland's influence on the gardens can still be seen. By acquiring all the remaining plots he preserved the earlier estate. The Temple became a pavilion for billiards and music for his guests. By 1818 he had created behind it a hidden Italian garden with a central pool and circular beds. From 1816 there were cricket and archery parties, and he hosted a wedding breakfast for 350 people for his son's wedding in 1826.

Copland and his gardener, Martin Doran, planted large numbers of trees, created a flower garden below the

ABOVE LEFT Alexander Copland (1774–1834). Miniature by W. J. Newton, 1828. Newton's son was apprenticed to Sydney Smirke, Copland's cousin.

ABOVE RIGHT Lucy Copland (1778–1849). Miniature by W. J. Newton, 1828.

ABOVE View across the lawn with the artist's stool and sketch books on the left. In the distance is the decorative five-arch bridge where the Horseshoe Pond was divided. Watercolour, about 1830.

Horseshoe Pond in 1810, bought more orange trees and installed glazed cast-iron cucumber frames in the recently acquired walled garden. The scale of their extensive greenhouses is shown by the loss of 3,600 squares of glass in a massive hailstorm one June evening in 1813.

Copland continued to extend and improve both his villa and the outbuildings. After he died in 1834 the sales particulars for the estate revealed his remarkably rich horticultural legacy, particularly of citrus trees. The purchaser in 1835 was the banker, Nathan Mayer Rothschild.

The Coplands were on good terms with the Morisons. Major Alexander Morison served in Bengal with the East India

Company and was still listed as 'of India' when he joined the Highland Society of London in 1807. He was 50 when he married Jane Carnell at St George's, Hanover Square in 1808, and was then described as 'of Gunnersbury House'.

While serving as a diplomat in London, future American president John Quincy Adams lived in Little Ealing and went to dinner with them all at Gunnersbury House on 12 October 1815: 'Major Morison is a Scotchman with the national attachments in all their force. There was music after dinner ... and Mrs Morison sang. The Major was enchanted with the Scotch songs.' Adams, Morison and Copland were members of a gentlemen's dining club at the New Inn in Ealing.

The Morisons' gardens were described in Loudon's *Gardener's Magazine* in 1827. From the grotto a stream of clear water ran over a pebbly bed to feed the Horseshoe Pond. In a separate building on the east side of the grotto wall was 'an ornamental dairy in the gothic style'.

William Johnstone Shennan, the gardener, cultivated orange trees, cactus and *Erythrina* or flame trees in the conservatory at the house. In the walled garden he was growing early peas and cabbages and the article emphasised his reputation for pineapples. Major Morison died in 1827 and Gunnersbury House was then sold to Thomas Farmer.

Thomas Farmer's family firm produced vitriol (sulphuric acid) in Kennington. Thomas, his wife Sarah and all their daughters held office in Wesleyan Methodist organisations. The Farmers set up and partly financed a Wesleyan day school for 50 girls in Acton in 1846.

Farmer's architects were the Pococks, father and son, whom he had met through their work for Methodist chapels. Farmer built new entrance gates and the East Lodge in 1837, improved the stabling in 1844, added the gothic screen and probably the open fernery on the north side of the grotto.

ABOVE Mr Shennan's boiler system, *The Gardener's Magazine*, 1827. Water from the Horseshoe Pond kept its reservoir topped up.

RIGHT Farmer extended the south side of the service (west) wing of Gunnersbury House to line up with the garden front of Cosser's 1802 villa. Photograph, about 1920.

BELOW Nathan and Hannah Rothschild in an oil painting portraying them with working papers. He oversaw the bank while she handled the business of home and family.

The mock ruins around his walled garden housed fruit store-rooms and gardeners' accommodation as well as hiding the neighbours' stables. After the house was severely damaged by fire in 1851 it was rebuilt with an enlarged west wing.

The Farmers' daughter, Elizabeth, inherited the estate in 1868 and married a banker, Henry John Atkinson, who had a passion for collecting early Bibles. The couple loved the gardens and from 1876 employed James Hudson as head gardener. They built glasshouses inside their stretch of the south wall of the 17th-century garden and from 1881 Hudson won prizes for the palms and tree ferns he grew there. The gardening press was impressed by the huge quantities of fruit and vegetables that he produced in the kitchen garden, vinery and pineapple house, and the plentiful supply of cut flowers for the house. In the 1880s Atkinson was an MP in Lincolnshire and sold Gunnersbury House to his neighbours, the Rothschilds, in August 1889.

Nathan Mayer Rothschild had married Hannah Barent Cohen in 1806 and established himself as a merchant banker

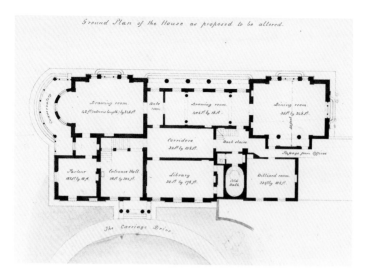

Ground Plan of the House as proposed to be altered.

in London in 1808. By the 1820s he was financier to the British government and many European states, with a town house at 107 Piccadilly. Hannah handled the purchase of Gunnersbury Park House in 1835 for £17,000. They bought the villa and its fixtures, the service buildings, 46½ acres of freehold and 29½ acres of leasehold land as well as the timber growing there.

They commissioned Sydney Smirke to enlarge the house and to design new stables. On the advice of J. C. Loudon they moved the entrance to make a grander drive from Popes Lane; Smirke now added an entrance portico to what had been the back of the North Lodge.

Though Nathan died in 1836, Hannah continued to improve the estate until her death 14 years later. She invested in more land including three large houses north of the park; by 1840 she owned 109 acres. Her primary interest remained the villa and the kitchen gardens. Since the estate quickly became famous for the exotic fruits which

ABOVE Although the Rothschilds purchased Copland's orangery, Smirke designed this new one against Maynard's wall by the Horseshoe Pond. Watercolour, about 1843.

enriched her table and made sumptuous gifts, she probably purchased the established plants in the walled garden from the Coplands.

Nathan Rothschild was not a showy man and scorned grand entertainments, but the more sophisticated Hannah saw that Gunnersbury could help the family play a more prominent role in society. When she had completed her improvements she held a 'Breakfast' for 500 guests, said to cost £2,000, in July 1838.

Some younger members of the family saw Hannah Rothschild as a formidable character but she was fun too.

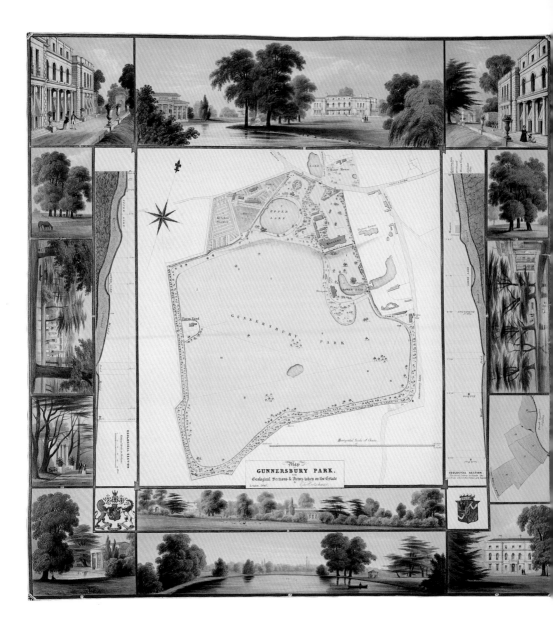

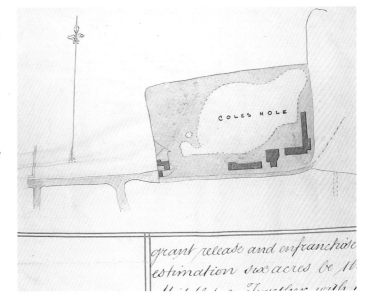

She was romping with her grandchildren in 1850 when she collapsed and died. Her £1.35 million fortune went to her four sons, all of whom already had country estates in Buckinghamshire. The younger brothers gave up their shares in Gunnersbury to Lionel, the eldest. He had been buying antique French furniture for the villa since the mid-1830s and hosting events for his political friends there in the 1840s. Benjamin Disraeli's barbed description of Gunnersbury to his sister was 'a villa worthy of an Italian prince though decorated with a taste and splendour which a French financier in olden times could alone have rivalled.' In 1857 Lionel and his wife Charlotte hosted at Gunnersbury the fabulously lavish wedding of their eldest daughter, Leonora, to her French cousin, followed by a banquet and an evening ball.

The family loved the gardens. The expert gardener, William Forsyth, grew huge quantities of fruit, including

6,000 pots of strawberry plants each summer and pineapples all year round; one variety was named after Charlotte. He provided decorative bedding schemes, potted plants for the terrace and cut flowers like the 200 sprigs of scented *Stephanotis* delivered in summer 1869 to the Piccadilly house. In the 1870s Charlotte's printed catalogue listed her 34 orchid varieties from around the world. Her son Leopold's gardeners maintained the collection and won a silver-gilt Royal Horticultural Society medal in 1898. The Gunnersbury orchids became the source of new varieties propagated by her grandson, Lionel, at Exbury.

ABOVE The polo players' mounting block, constructed of brick with stone cappings, near the sports field.

Lionel de Rothschild spent considerable sums in the 1850s and 1860s converting leases into freehold land and adding another 331 acres. In 1861 he bought the pottery and its clay pit known as Coles Hole, which became the Potomac Lake. With the kiln converted as a gothic tower boathouse, artificial Pulhamite rocks, huge trees moved from elsewhere in the grounds, new shrubberies and clumps of bamboos and pampas grass, this became a picturesque spot. He also bought Brentford Common Field (today's sports field), demolished his long west estate wall and upgraded the model farm in a pretty gothick style. The farmland was worked for the next 50 years, providing pasture for fattening cattle and a hay crop.

Lionel and Charlotte's third son, Leopold, shared his father's enthusiasm for horses. The field also provided space for the horses of the Gunnersbury stud which they began in the 1860s. In 1879 their horse, Sir Bevys, won the Derby only days before Lionel died. Now Leopold and his wife Marie inherited Gunnersbury. He became a well-known racing personality, described in 1904 in the *Middlesex County Times* as 'the most popular owner on the Turf next to his Majesty'. From about 1910 part of the field became a polo pitch for the private club run by Evelyn de Rothschild, one of Leopold's sons, who was killed in action in Palestine in 1917. Another son, Lionel, has left us a fine photographic record, including some rare colour images using the autochrome process.

In 1889 Leopold bought the Atkinsons' Gunnersbury House, bringing the old estate back into single ownership, though most of the dividing wall was not demolished for a decade. Having inherited his mother's love of gardening, Leopold asked the famous Mr Hudson to continue to

manage the garden and together they set to work on new projects.

Leopold and Hudson's major project in 1900 was the Japanese Garden, north of Smirke's stables. Designed with miniature banks and islands linked by narrow watercourses (some warmed, some cool), bamboo bridges and stepping stones, Hudson sought far and wide for plants of Chinese and Japanese origin. It was opened by the Japanese ambassador, who commented diplomatically that nothing like it had been seen in Japan. They created a Wall Garden using planting niches in the mock ruins, a bamboo garden and a garden of heathers planted in 1906. Both Hudson and George Reynolds, Forsyth's successor in the larger garden, were very prominent in the gardening press.

Leopold followed the family tradition of a lively social life at Gunnersbury. Cricket matches and garden parties supported local charities. Other events were much grander, like the League of Mercy Garden Party in aid of King Edward VII's Fund in 1912 attended by 2,000 guests, including George V and Queen Mary and many members of the aristocracy.

ABOVE Lionel was a passionate motoring enthusiast. This photograph, taken on the Terrace in 1902, shows him at the wheel of his 6½ horsepower Bardon.

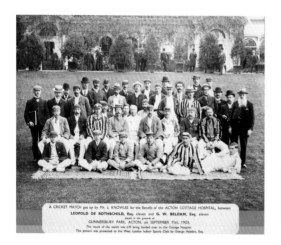

A CRICKET MATCH got up by Mr. J. KNOWLES for the Benefit of the ACTON COTTAGE HOSPITAL, between **LEOPOLD DE ROTHSCHILD**, Esq. eleven and **G. W. BELDAM**, Esq. eleven played in the grounds of GUNNERSBURY PARK, ACTON, on SEPTEMBER 11th, 1903. The result of the match was £70 being handed over to the Cottage Hospital. This picture was presented to the West London Indoor Sports Club by George Hebben, Esq.

GUNNERSBURY PARK.

In the 1890s Leopold and his brother Nathaniel began developing land in Ealing for suburban housing, and they sold land to the south for the new Brentford Market. After Leopold died in May 1917 his eldest son, Lionel, inherited Gunnersbury but it was no longer such a desirable place. In 1919 Lionel bought Exbury in the New Forest where he created a very fine garden. An Act of Parliament for the building of the Great West Road was passed in 1914 but work did not start until 1920. The new road bypassing overcrowded Brentford ran across Rothschild land to the south. It opened in 1925, making the Gunnersbury estate very valuable for housing and industrial development, so it was put up for sale.

RIGHT In the early 1900s the Rothschilds grew a substantial mushroom crop in the surviving cellars of the 17th century house.

OPPOSITE LEFT The teams from a charity cricket match at Gunnersbury in 1903, which raised £70 for the Acton Cottage Hospital. Photographed on the lawn below the Small Mansion.

OPPOSITE RIGHT Kitchen and household staff in 1914 when the Rothschilds were in residence.

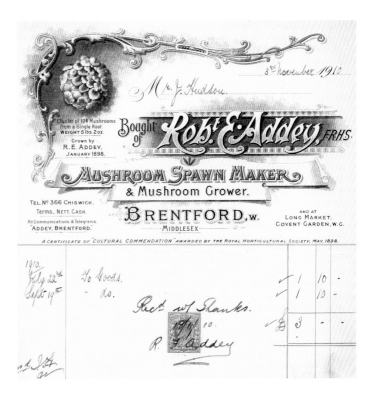

'ANOTHER LUNG FOR LONDON'

(British Pathé news film of opening ceremony)

The Public Park

In 1920 the then Borough of Ealing offered £500 an acre to create a park on Rothschild land in Ealing, north of Popes Lane. Local people, from the Middle Classes Union to the Labour Party, objected mainly on the grounds of cost. The Ministry of Health held a public inquiry, decided Ealing did not need another park and refused to sanction the necessary loan. The proposal was dropped.

Five years later the Borough of Ealing decided to buy Gunnersbury Park in Brentford. The Mayor of Acton proposed a joint purchase with Ealing; it lay on the boundary of both their boroughs and would greatly benefit their residents. Again, there was vociferous local opposition, including from Brentford Urban District Council.

After another public inquiry the purchase went ahead. The Councils successfully pressed for a reduction in price from £150,000 to £125,000 (£625 per acre) and even asked the Rothschild bank for a mortgage towards the cost!

OPPOSITE The grand opening of the Park, May 1926, with dignitaries in the foreground. Wakefields were the official photographers and Ealing's Walpole Cinema made a newsreel.

A 25 per cent loan from Middlesex County Council enabled the purchase to go ahead in December 1925, with permission to sell house plots along the full lengths of Popes Lane and Lionel Road to reimburse the cost. Ealing and Acton believed that sufficient income could be raised through sports and other facilities to cover the running costs. Brentford lost its chance to build houses and levy rates on all the land.

A joint management committee was created, with councillors from both boroughs. They invited the Urban Districts of Brentford and Chiswick to join the board. Neither could afford it at first but they joined in 1927. The committee appointed a superintendent, a deputy and a team of gardeners and park-keepers, 36 staff in all. Bids came in

THE
PUBLIC HEALTH ACT, 1875.

EALING & ACTON.

WHEREAS the Councils of the Boroughs of Ealing and Acton have applied to the Minister of Health for sanction to borrow the sums of £51,070 and £45,342 respectively towards the cost of acquiring Gunnersbury Park as an open space, and the Minister of Health has directed Inquiry into the subject-matter of such Application :

NOTICE IS HEREBY GIVEN that M. K. North, Esq., M.Inst.C.E., the Inspector appointed to hold the said inquiry, will attend for that purpose at the Town Hall, Ealing, on Tuesday, the Twelfth day of May, 1925, at Half-past Eleven o'clock in the Forenoon, and will then and there be prepared to receive the evidence of any persons interested in the matter of the said Inquiry.

I. G. GIBBON,
Assistant Secretary.

Ministry of Health,
April 27th, 1925.

OPPOSITE Charles Smith, the horse-keeper appointed in 1935, with horse-drawn cart number 3.

OPPOSITE BELOW Announcement of the public inquiry in 1925 which resulted in the purchase of the estate.

BELOW The Popes Lane gate, with traders selling ices and fruit to visitors. Postcard, late 1920s.

from people wishing to offer boat hire, fishing and golf, and requests for such events as Scout camps and Metropolitan Mounted Police displays – even for use of the field for an air display. The walled gardens were leased out for horticulture and by the spring of 1926 the owner of 500 sheep had hired the field for grazing. The Rothschilds sold 16 second-hand mowing machines and six turf rollers and also offered 'two old coaches of historical interest' which are now part of the Museum collection.

The Joint Committee borrowed £7,000 to transform the estate into a public park. Besides the 100 park benches, litter bins and railings, garden tools, plants and seeds, drinking fountains and public lavatories, they set up sports facilities

GUNNERSBURY PARK, POPES LANE MAIN ENTRANCE   61006

and offered golf, putting, tennis, football, cricket, hockey, netball, rugby, fishing, bowling and paddleboats.

From this time the two villas began to be called the Small Mansion and the Large Mansion. Mrs Bridger, who ran tea rooms at Battersea Park, paid £170 annually for a contract to provide high-class catering in the former and 'more popular' teas at the Farm and Stables.

Neville Chamberlain, Minister of Health, performed the opening ceremony shortly before the 1926 May Bank Holiday weekend. The superintendent reported 'crowds large on Saturday, tremendous on Sunday and overwhelming on Monday', totalling 60,000 to 100,000. Visitors were excited to explore high-quality gardens, without the kind of restrictions imposed at Kew Gardens, and enjoy the sports.

New entrances were created in Popes Lane and at its corner with Lionel Road. Low walls topped by iron railings mark the point where the corner of the park was taken for the North Circular Road. The Large Mansion was repaired in 1927 and a museum subcommittee began seeking local antiquities. The museum opened in September 1929 using three ground-floor rooms. Councillor Miss Susan Smee, former Mayor of Acton, was honorary curator until the outbreak of war.

Some staff went to fight, but enough remained to form a Home Guard unit. A newsletter shared information about those on active service. The museum displays were packed away. Sand was quarried 'for Civil Defence purposes'

ABOVE The last hay crop gathered from the big field in 1920. Mr Swansel, the foreman in the bowler hat, with his workers beside the haystack.

and between 1940 and 1943 the upper part of the field, surrounded by barbed wire, housed a heavy anti-aircraft artillery site. Its substantial concrete footings were traced by archaeologists in 2014.

The post-war park slowly recovered. The councils filled and capped the sandpit (dug for sandbags) in the south-east corner of the park. The Pavilion Café replaced the tea room in the Small Mansion in 1958, flats were made for park staff in the upper floors of the mansions, the 22 football pitches

BELOW Members of the 71st Middlesex Home Guard Heavy Anti-Aircraft Battery, Royal Artillery, photographed at Gunnersbury in 1944.

FRANK MILLS 2nd ROW FROM TOP.
THIRD FROM RIGHT

WAKEFIELDS EALING 1000

"B" TROOP
71st MIDDX. H.G. H.A.A. BATTERY
JUNE 1944.

were popular at the weekends, but the rise in car ownership began to offer families days out far from the park.

When the new London Boroughs of Ealing and Hounslow were created in 1965 six councillors from each served on the management committee. In the 1960s they set up a Training Centre for London parks staff and a Teachers' Centre in the Small Mansion. Having pulled down some decaying 18th-century buildings including a dairy near the café they proposed demolishing the Temple in 1971. The Greater London Council refused permission and grant-aided its restoration in 1973. The Stables, deemed beyond repair, were offered to a developer in 1981 for conversion into offices. The museum would have lost its long-hoped-for scheme to turn them into a home for its carriages and large exhibits. The groundswell of opposition created the Friends of Gunnersbury Park & Museum. Amongst other things, its volunteers set up a riding school and restored the Victorian kitchens.

The last 30 years have seen successes and difficulties. The derelict Orangery was restored through a planning deal with a developer, an arts group moved into the Small Mansion

ABOVE LEFT Some of the extensive glasshouses in the nursery in 1960, which supplied plants for Hounslow Council open spaces until 1993.

ABOVE RIGHT Leopold de Rothschild's farm buildings had picturesque thatch and rustic columns before they became the sports changing rooms. Photograph, 1960.

with studios and a gallery, and the new Heritage Lottery Fund helped restore the Italian Gardens, the setting of the Round Pond, Amelia's grotto and the lamp standards on the main drive. Regeneration money paid for a new children's playground. Capel Manor, London's horticultural college, established its West London base in the 18th-century walled garden in 1994.

RIGHT, TOP & BOTTOM The stables and the orangery in 1981.

Many people remember the Queen's Golden Jubilee visit in 2002, and the lively annual Mela festival started in 2003. But it was a struggle to maintain even the occupied buildings and the grounds, and lack of maintenance and arson in the changing rooms almost put an end to the sports activity. The East Lodge fell in and no solution was found for the Stables. There was never a year when both Boroughs together could find extra funding, but there were many when

ABOVE London's Dhol Academy performing in the finale of the 2017 London Mela. This Asian-themed festival for all was launched by the Mayor of London in 2003.

one or the other had to reduce the budget. Gunnersbury was always quite high up the 'Heritage at Risk' register.

The problems were easy to see, the solutions were rather harder to find. But everyone loves their parks; they are places full of treasured memories. Local people stayed engaged with Gunnersbury's difficulties. The elements of a way forward emerged – political will, commitment to shared funding, restoration in phases, fundraising, new governance, Lottery support for both preparing the plans and then delivering them. The target became restoration in time for the Park centenary – 'Gunnersbury 2026'.

In a £21 million first phase the Large Mansion has been restored: the local history museum for the London Boroughs of Ealing and Hounslow now occupies all of the building. The Café has been rebuilt with a space for the carriages alongside. In the gardens historic walls and arches, the Temple, Orangery, main entrance and grotto area have been restored. Removing the railing around the old golf course has opened up the centre of the park. Historic views have been emphasised, a Kitchen Garden has been planted. Half the Horseshoe Pond has been recreated and the Round Pond has been made watertight using clay dug from the Victoria & Albert Museum's new basement. Fresh planting, nature trails, a new small playground and unusual sculptures from the timber of fallen trees enhance the grounds. Investment in new sports facilities will revitalise the field and offer benefits to many people from a wide area. Full restoration will follow in further phases.

In its long history Gunnersbury has been transformed by Maynard, Furnese and Amelia, Morley and Copland, the Rothschilds and the making of a public park. Each transformation has left traces in the landscape. 'Gunnersbury 2026' is the transformation for our generation.

This edition © Scala Arts & Heritage Publishers Ltd, 2018

Text © Val Bott and James Wisdom, 2018

First published in 2018 by
Scala Arts & Heritage Publishers Ltd
10 Lion Yard, Tremadoc Road
London SW4 7NQ
United Kingdom

www.scalapublishers.com

In association with the Friends of Gunnersbury Park & Museum

gunnersburyfriends.org

ISBN 978-1-78551-132-5

Edited by Hannah Bowen
Designed by Andrew Barron
Printed and bound in Turkey

10 9 8 7 6 5 4 3 2 1

Front cover: A summer's day by the Horseshoe Pond. Tempera on canvas by Maxwell Ashby Armfield, first exhibited 1933.

Front cover flap: John Rocque's map of *London and Environs*, 1746.

Inside front cover: A carriage arriving at the north entrance of Gunnersbury House showing the stables on the left and the domestic service wing on the right. Watercolour by William Payne, 1792.

Back cover: The mansion from the Horseshoe Pond, after lawns had replaced the formal gardens. Watercolour by William Payne, 1792.

Back cover flap: RAF aerial photograph of the Park with anti-aircraft gun emplacements and barrack huts at the top of the field, 7 August 1944.

Inside back cover: Gunnersbury Park House, with the first of the rose basket beds (left). The Burmese bell hanging between the trees summoned guests for tea. Watercolour, late 1830s. Photo © National Trust.

Every effort has been made to acknowledge correct copyright of images where applicable. Any errors or omissions are unintentional and should be notified to the Publisher, who will arrange for corrections to appear in any reprints.

We are grateful to the following for permission to use images from their collections:

Michael Copland-Griffiths: pages 23, 26 (left and right), 27

Ealing Council Legal Services: pages 15 (bottom left), 25, 33, 40 (bottom)

Stephanie (Cosser) Farnsworth: page 24 (top right)

Ken Finding: page 43

Victor Frankowski: page 46

Gunnersbury Park Museum: Front and back covers, inside front cover, pages 1, 3, 8 (top), 9, 13, 15 (top right), 20, 21 (bottom right), 36 (bottom left), 39, 40 (top), 41, 42, 44 (left and right)

Historic England Archive (RAF Photography): Back cover flap

Hounslow Local History & Archives: pages 17, 19 (left and right)

Lewis Walpole Library, Yale University: page 18 (left and right)

London Metropolitan Archives/COLLAGE: page 7 (bottom left)

Museum of Fine Arts Boston, Augustus Hemenway and Arthur William Wheelwright Fund 40.89: page 14

National Trust Images: page 6

Private Collection: pages 28–29

The Rothschild Archive, London: pages 30, 31, 35 (left and right), 36 (top), 36 (bottom right), 37

Royal Collection Trust: pages 4 (top), 16, 32

Royal Society: page 4 (bottom)

Thomas Layton Collection: page 7 (top right)

Waddesdon (National Trust) Dorothy de Rothschild Bequest 1988, acc. no. 2855. Photo: Mike Fear © National Trust, Waddesdon Manor: Inside back cover

Yale Centre for British Art, Paul Mellon Collection: page 24 (bottom left)

The authors wish to record their thanks to:

The historians who have shared their research: Jan Anderson, David Bush, Paul Fitzmaurice and Chris Hern

Toni Marshall (Medioto), Peter Hughes (Photoview), Jonathan Hurwitt (photography), Melanie Aspey (The Rothschild Archive, London), James Marshall and team (Hounslow Local History & Archives), Susie Batchelor, Julia Tubman and Amy Dobson (Gunnersbury Park Museum; visitgunnersbury.org), Vanda Foster, former Museum Curator, and Mike Rowan, former Park Manager at Gunnersbury

The Friends of Gunnersbury Park & Museum and the John & Ruth Howard Charitable Trust, whose funding made this publication possible.